AMERICA
Salt & Pepper Shakers

Sylvia Tompkins & Irene Thornburg

4880 Lower Valley Road, Atglen, PA 19310 USA

Designed by Bonnie M. Hensley
Type set in Van Dijk/Korinna BT

ISBN: 0-7643-1126-3
Printed in China
1 2 3 4

Published by Schiffer Publishing Ltd.
4880 Lower Valley Road
Atglen, PA 19310
Phone: (610) 593-1777; Fax: (610) 593-2002
E-mail: Schifferbk@aol.com
Please visit our web site catalog at **www.schifferbooks.com**
We are always looking for people to write books on new and related subjects. If you have an idea for a
book, please contact us at the above address.

This book may be purchased from the publisher. Include $3.95 for shipping. Please try your book-
store first. You may write for a free catalog.

In Europe, Schiffer books are distributed by:
Bushwood Books
6 Marksbury Ave.
Kew Gardens
Surrey TW9 4JF
England
Phone: 44 (0)208 392-8585
Fax: 44 (0)208 392-9876
E-mail: Bushwd@aol.com
Free postage in the UK. Europe: air mail at cost. Try your bookstore first.

Contents

Acknowledgments

We sincerely appreciate the assistance and encouragement of friends and collectors, and especially the following contributors to this book: Wyona Braun, Larry Carey, Quent Christman, Eva and Chuck Drometer, Harvey Duke, Gayette Fratzke, Dot Gammon, Pat Glascock, Marty Grossman, Mike Hall, Irene Harms, Lorraine Haywood, Betty and Freddie Hunter, Wendy Johnston, Grant Karr, Heath Karr, Sharon and Ralph Karr, Mike Kaul, Jeanne Langer, Phil Mays, Kandi and Gary Mitchell, Jean Moon, Richland County Historical Society Museum in Wapheton, North Dakota, Joanne Rose, Diana and Larry Sanderson, Marcia Smith, and The Geographical Center Pioneer Village and Museum in Rugby, North Dakota.

We want to thank Betty and Freddie Hunter for their major contributions to our book. We enjoyed their hospitality and their fabulous collection. The opportunity to take photographs of their sets and their input on prices have been invaluable.

Introduction

In the beginning, most collectors acquired salt and pepper sets because they were appealing, a souvenir from a trip, received as a gift, or simply because they had holes in the top. Through the years, as collections have grown, their owners have wanted to learn more about the origin and background of various sets.

Interest has been steadily growing in American made salt and pepper shakers, and although books have been written on some American pottery companies, salt and pepper shakers were not the primary focus. We are presenting sets here that are from lesser known manufacturers as well as sets made by familiar companies. Due to an increased interest in North Dakota pottery, we are featuring Rosemeade, Messer, and other North Dakota potteries.

The Rosemeade Price Guide by Bill Bakken includes Rosemeade prices from the North Dakota Pottery Collectors Society, commercial, and Internet auctions during the last three years. These prices plus input from contributors have been averaged to arrive at the Rosemeade values included in this book. Values for other sets are based on input from contributors and our experience. As always, values are intended only as a guide. These values will vary based on condition, geographical location, knowledge of the seller and buyer, and, sometimes, pure luck.

Plans for a future book include sets made by Regal China, Margaret Weese, Billie Vier, Treasure Craft, Twin Winton, Shirley, Rick Wisecarver, and others.

The Novelty Salt and Pepper Shakers Club is an international organization of 1,400 members. These collectors enjoy the friendships and benefits derived from joining with others who share a love of their hobby. Twenty-one regional chapters (eighteen U.S. and three Canadian) afford an opportunity for collectors to get together with others in their area. Each year the Club convention is held in a different part of the country to give as many members as possible a chance to attend. Quarterly newsletters provide information on shaker identification and history, as well as a means to buy, sell, and trade. For more information about the Club, please contact the authors.

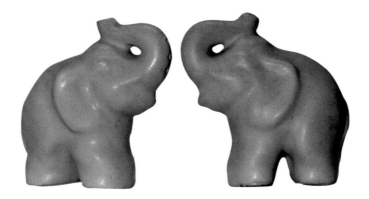

North Dakota Potteries

Rosemeade

Rosemeade pottery was manufactured from 1940 to 1961 by the Wapheton Pottery Company in North Dakota, owned by Laura Taylor Hughes and Robert Hughes. This pottery was named for Rosemeade Township where Laura lived, and for the pink wild prairie roses which are the North Dakota state flower. The clay used, which came primarily from beds near Mandan, North Dakota, had a distinctive rosy-beige color and character. For a short time during the 1950s, the company experimented with a white clay from Kentucky. However, use of this clay was limited. Glazes include high gloss, matte finish, and a metallic-bronze. Among the many wildlife subjects portrayed were various pheasants, a favorite of Laura Hughes. In addition to the many salt and pepper shakers shown in this book, the company also made figurines, ash trays, spoon rests, lamps, sugar and creamer sets, wall plaques, vases, etc. During its years of operation, the factory gave tours for school children and unfinished pieces were given to the children to take home and decorate. Most sets were issued with the Rosemeade prairie rose label. Some are stamped "Rosemeade" or "North Dakota Rosemeade."

Visit with Irene Harms

In June 1999, we were privileged to visit Irene Harms, co-author of the book *Beautiful Rosemeade*, in her South Dakota home. Irene started collecting salt and pepper shakers in high school. As her interest grew, she realized a need to focus her collection on a more specific area. She especially liked her three sets of Rosemeade: pheasants, skunks, and fish on tails. Subsequently, she acquired several Rosemeade figurines at a museum auction, plus seventy-nine pairs of salt and peppers at $3.00 a set (we should all be so lucky!). This determined her collecting focus. In the 1980s, Shirley Sampson approached Irene about co-authoring a book on Rosemeade. As a joint venture, Shirley did the pictures and Irene was responsible for the writing and printing. They had their book signing at Wapheton in 1986.

Salt and pepper shaker set commemorating the tenth anniversary of the North Dakota Pottery Collectors Society in 1999 (not made by Rosemeade). Issue price $20.

Color Blocks. Several colors were used in Rosemeade production. Variations exist, however, and not every set will exactly match the color shown.

Pheasant mold before and after firing, showing reduction in size due to clay shrinkage.

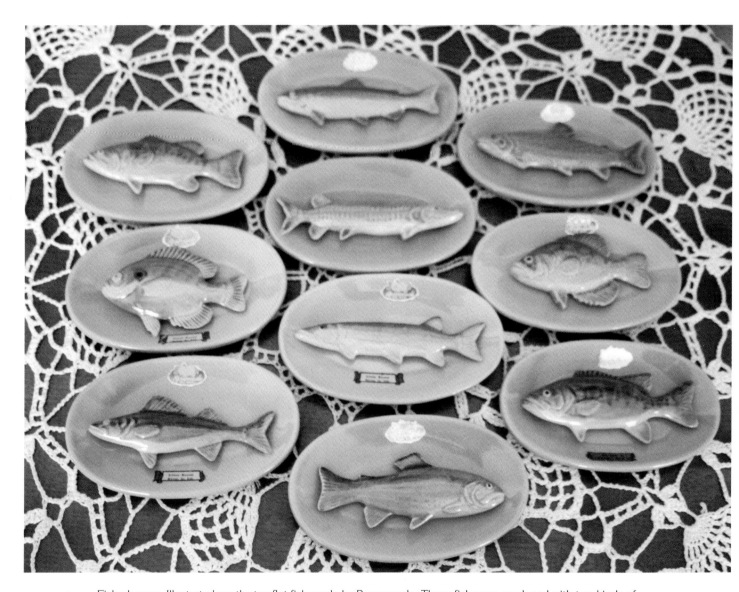

Fish plaques. Illustrated are the ten flat fish made by Rosemeade. These fish were produced with two kinds of bottoms: totally flat with the fish name incised, and with a raised edge or ridge. The completely flat bottoms were used on the wall plaques. Some of these were also produced as salt and peppers. However, the majority of the flat fish shakers were probably made with the ridge, as very few of the others have surfaced to date.

BEATIFUL  GIFTWARE

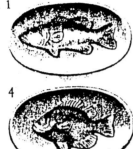

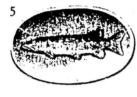

FISH WALL PLAQUES for Hanging

ILLUSTRATED

1—Large Mouthed Bass   5—Northern Pike
2—Muskellunge   6—Crappie
3—Brook Trout   7—Walloye
4—Bluegill   8—Small Mouthed Bass

NOT ILLUSTRATED

9—Rainbow Trout   10—Salmon

You have never seen more natural looking pottery fish than the ten varieties listed above. The coloring is realistic too, and the fish are mounted on sea green platters which are designed for hanging.

We also have SALT and PEPPER SETS in the ten fish listed above.

Fish Wall Plaque—3½x6" . . . . Price Each 90¢
Fish Salt and Pepper Sets . . . . Per Pair 90¢

ROSEMEADE POTTERIES
WAHPETON, NORTH DAKOTA

POST CARD

GENUINE CURTEICH-CHICAGO "C.T. ART-COLORTONE" POST CARD (REG. U.S. PAT. OFF.)

PLACE
STAMP
HERE

2C-N847

9

Badgers. 1.25". $600+.

Miniature bears. 2". $125-150.

Bears with one arm out, one down. 3.5". $55-65.

Bears with both arms out. 3.5". $55-65.

Bears with both arms down. 3". $55-65.

Bears with both arms down, showing
color contrast. 3". $55-65.

Jayhawks. 2.5". $500+.

Jayhawk cheerleaders. 2.25". $600+.

Robins and bluebirds. 1.75". $175-200.

Goldfinches. 1.25". $125-150. Chickadees. 1.25". $225-250.

Parrots. 2.75". $100-125

Parakeets. 2.5". $175-200.

Eagles. 3". $300+.

Doves. 2". $225-250.

Flamingos. 4". $125-150.

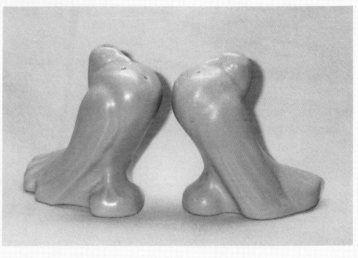

Both Pages
Strutting Pigeons. 3.5". Rust with gold
accent $300+; others $250-275.

Pelicans. 3". $50-60.

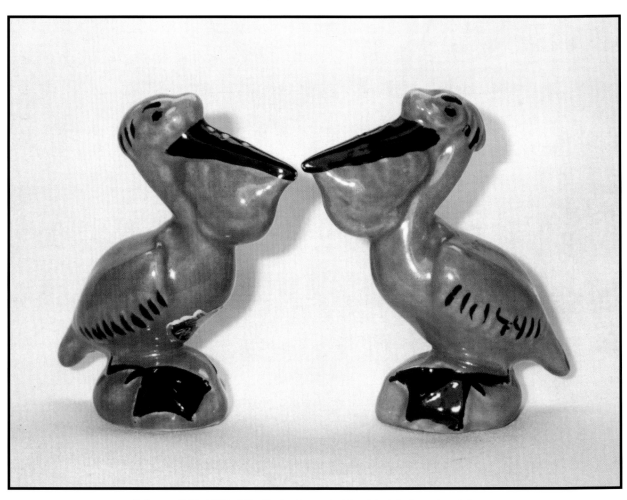

Pelicans. 3.5". $100-125. Black trim probably added during a lunch hour.

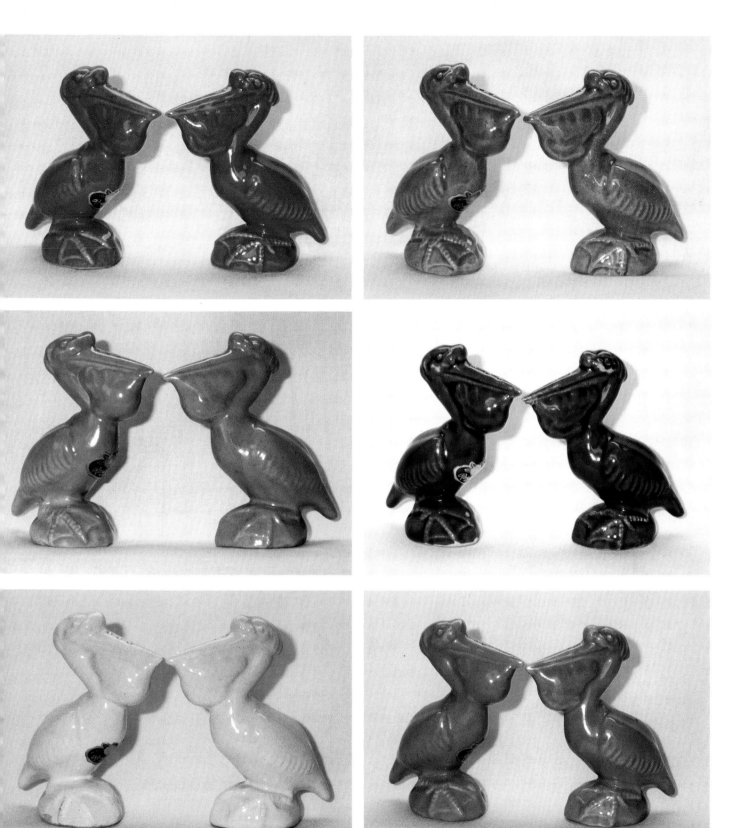

Pelicans. 3.5". $65-75.

Bison. 2.5". $100-115.

Siamese cats. 2.75". $75-85.

Siamese cats with dark blue trim. 2.75". $90-100.

Black cats. 2.75". $55-65.

Cats. 3.25". $55-65.

Walking kittens. 2.5". $100-115.

Oxen. 2.25". $75-85.

Cow and bull. 2". Pearlized white with gold trim $300+; others $200+.

Brahmas. 1.75". $400+.

Large rooster and hen with chick,
pearlized white with gold trim.
3.75". $400+.

Large rooster and hen with
chick, white. 3.75". $300+.

Large chickens. 3.5". $100-115.

Fighting cocks. 3.75". $150-175.

Svelte chickens. 3.5". $40-45.

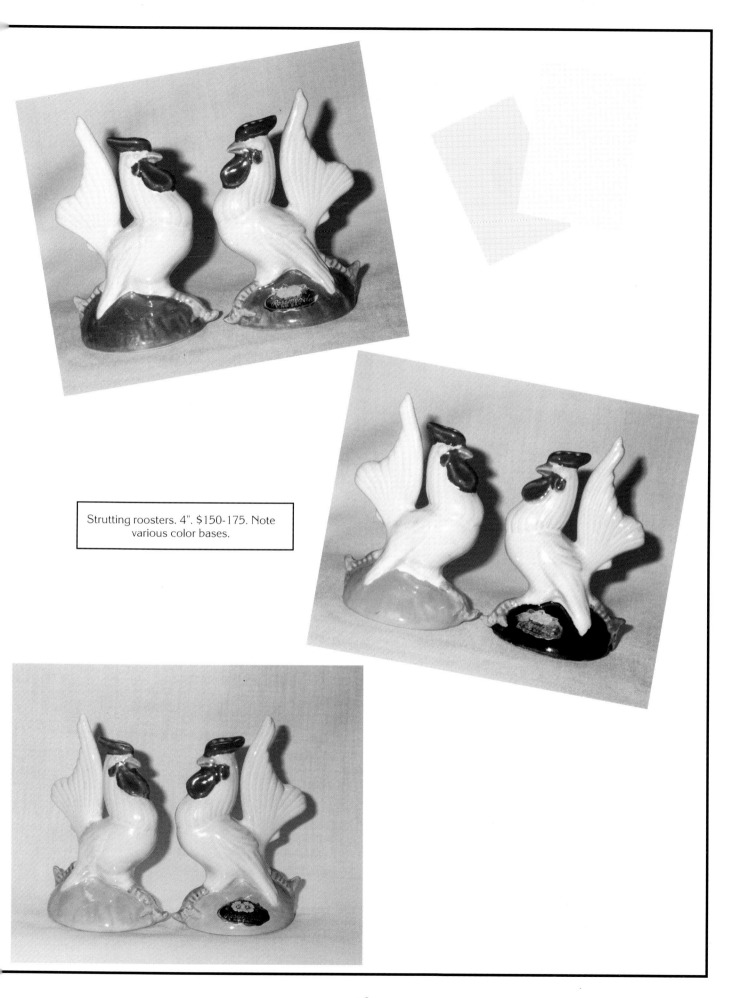

Strutting roosters. 4". $150-175. Note
various color bases.

Small chickens. 3". $75-85.

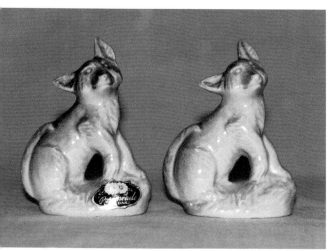

Sitting coyotes. 3". $275-300.

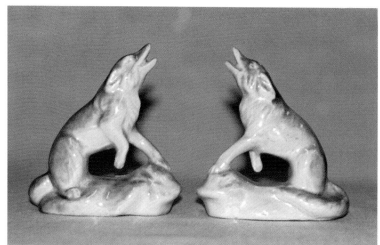

Howling coyotes. 3". $250-275.

Leaping deer. 3.5". $75-85.

Fawns. 2.25". $65-75.

Pointers. 2.25". $900+.

Begging dogs. 3". $50-60.

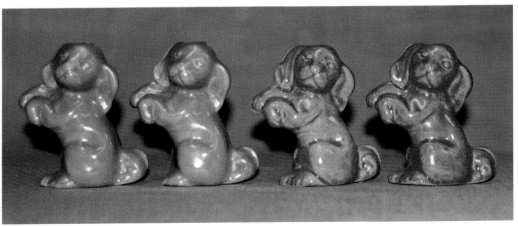

Cocker spaniels. 2". $175-200.

Cocker spaniels. 2.25". $175-200.

Cocker spaniel singles. 2.25" and 2".
Shows size comparison. Not priced.

Boston Terriers. 2.5". $225-250. Wire Haired Fox Terriers with two-tone brown ears. 2". $40-50.

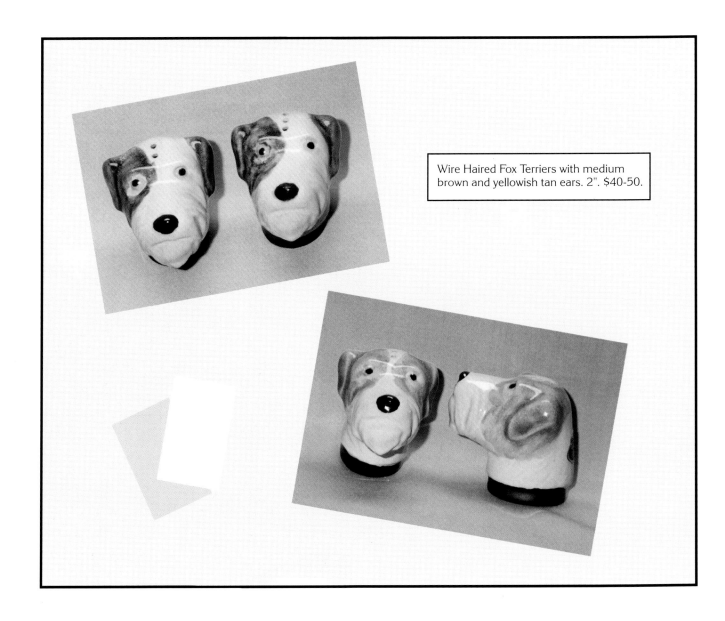

Wire Haired Fox Terriers with medium brown and yellowish tan ears. 2". $40-50.

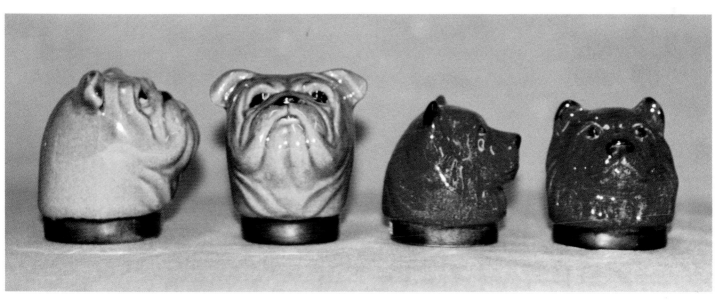

English Bull Dogs. 2.5". $80-90. Chow Chows. 2". $50-60.

Chow Chows. 2". $50-60.

Bloodhounds. 3". $60-70. Greyhounds. 2.5". $40-50.

Dalmatians. 2.75". $90-100. English Setters. 2.75". $40-50.

English Toy Terriers (also known as English Toy Spaniels). 2". $40-50. Pekingese. 1.75". $80-90.

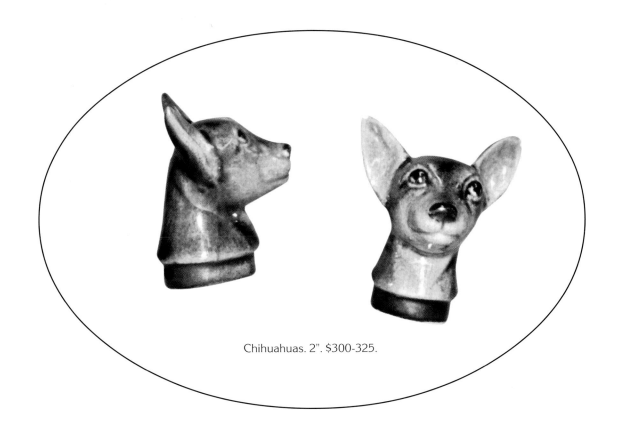

Chihuahuas. 2". $300-325.

Scottish Terriers with red tongue. 2.75". $70-80. Scottish Terriers. 2.5". $40-50.

Donkeys on horseshoes. 3". Rare, museum piece. Not priced..

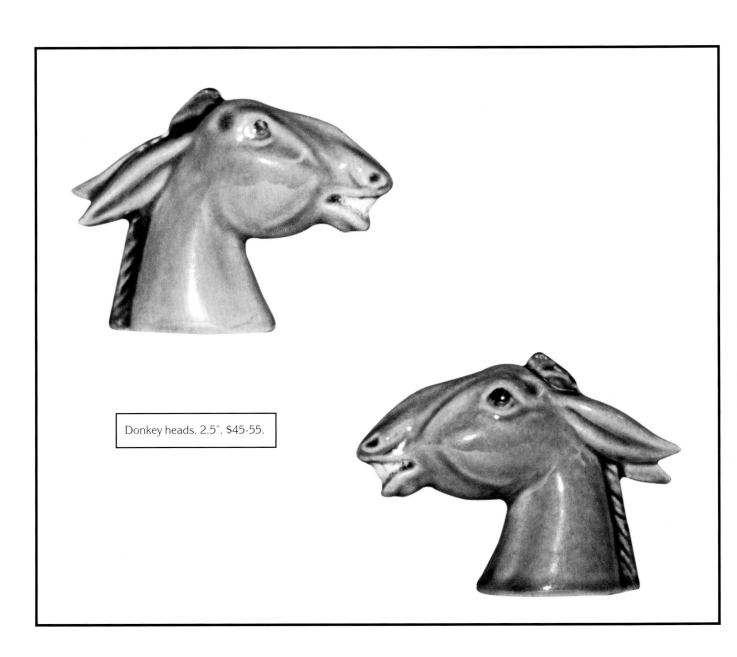

Donkey heads. 2.5". $45-55.

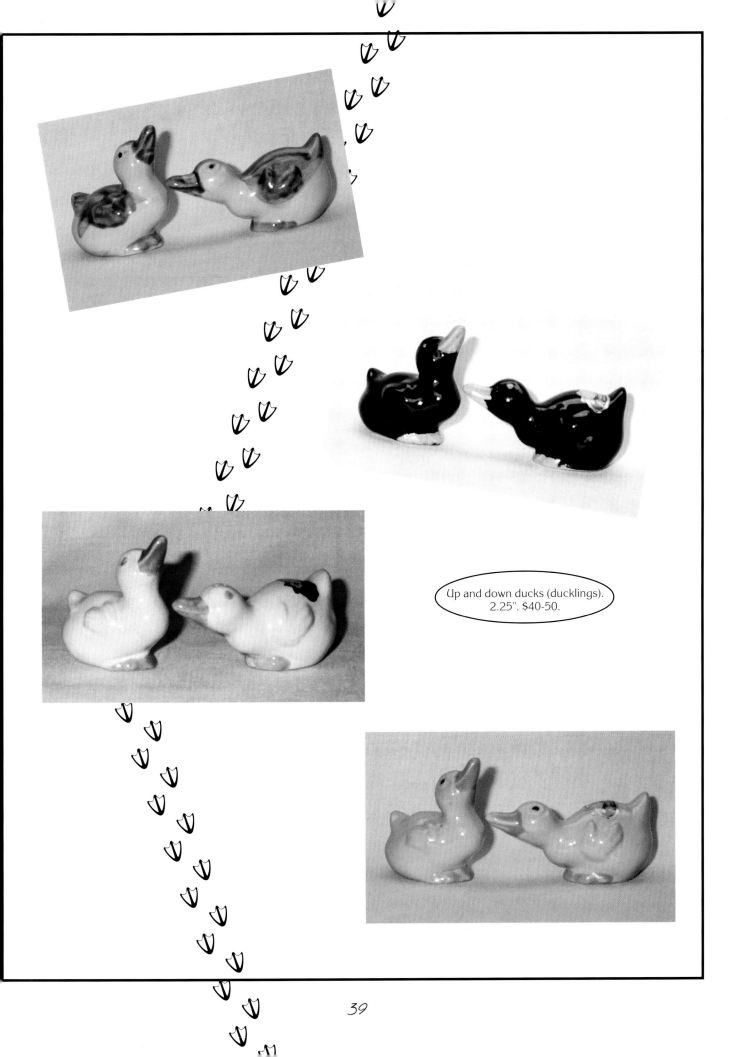

Up and down ducks (ducklings).
2.25". $40-50.

Miniature mallards. 1". $225-250.

Fargo Forum ducks. 2.5". Given as a promotion by the Fargo Forum, a shoe store in Fargo, North Dakota. $600+.

Set made for the town of Black Duck, Minnesota. 2". Probably made as an advertising or souvenir set. $400+.

Mallards. 3.5". $55-65.

Mallard drakes. 3.5".
$75-85. Made with
two and three holes.

Both Pages
Elephants. 2.75". Metallic dark
gray $90-100; others $55-65.

Elephants with white tusks. 2.75". $65-75.

Elephants with white tusks. 2.75". $65-75.

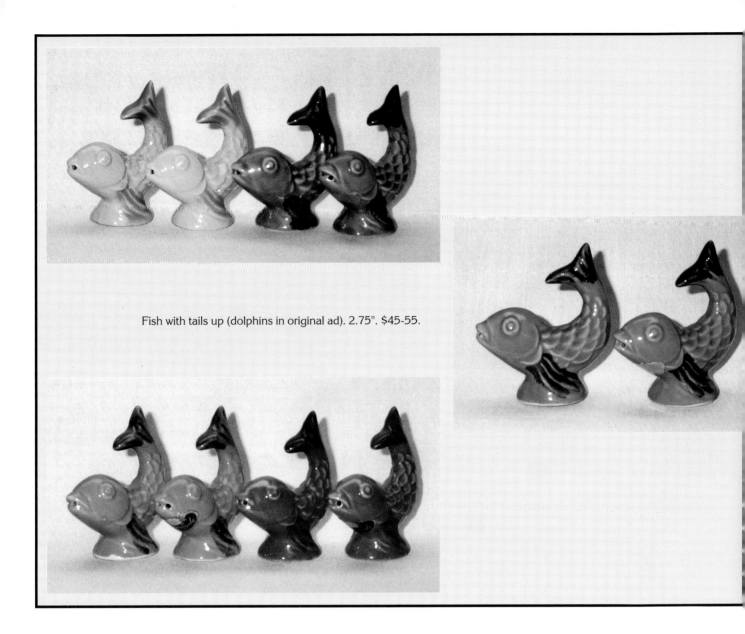

Fish with tails up (dolphins in original ad). 2.75". $45-55.

Sailfish. 4.25". $225-250.

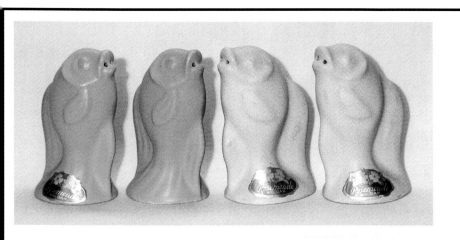

Fish on tails. 2.75". $60-70.

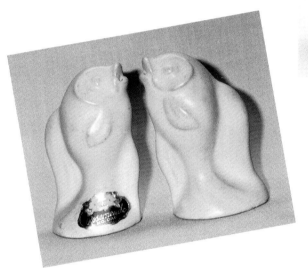

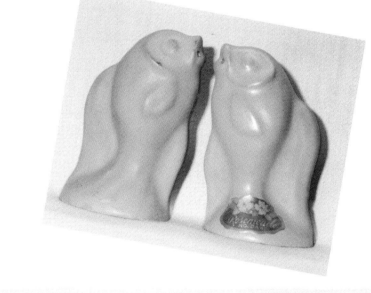

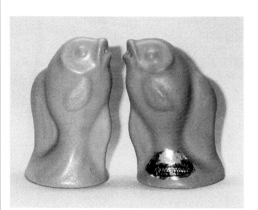

Rainbow trout. 1.5". $425-450.

Catfish. 1.5". $700+.

Bullheads. 1.5". $700+.

Salmon. .75". $900+.

Blue Gills. .75". $475-500.

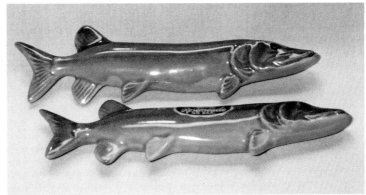

Northern Pike. .75". $500-525.

Muskellunge. .75". Flat back. $650-675.

Muskellunge. .75". Ridge back. $600-625.

51

Smooth Crappies. .75". Ridge back $400-425; flat back $450-475.

Crappies with scales. .75". $400-425.

Rainbow Trout. .75". $800+.

Brown Trout. .75". Ridge back $400-425; flat back $475-500.

Large Mouth Bass. .75". $500-525.

Small Mouth Bass above, Large Mouth Bass below. .75". Shows difference in fins. Not priced.

Small Mouth Bass. .75". $500-525.

Walleye. .75". $500-525.

Flickertails. 2.25". $65-75.

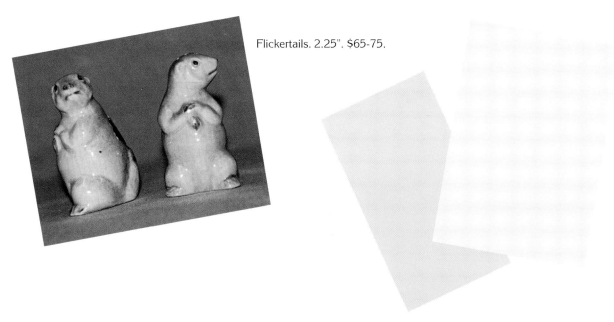

Foxes. 1.75". $400-425.

Mountain goats. 2". $175-200.

Mountain goats. 2". Decorated by a
school child. Not priced.

Gophers. Left set 4.25". $90-100. Right set 3.25". $75-85.

Gophers. 3.25". $150-175.
Note bluish color.

57

Horse heads. 2.25". $75-85.

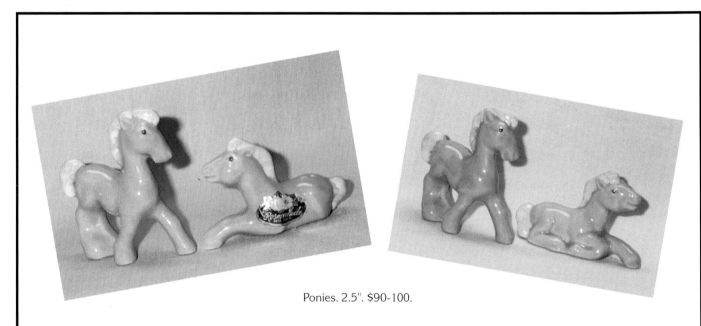

Ponies. 2.5". $90-100.

Kangaroos. 3.25". $60-70.

Mice. 2". $55-65.

Kangaroo family. 2.75". $300-325.

Miniature pheasants. 2.25". $325-350.

Crouched pheasants. 1.75". $100-125.

Pheasants with tails up. Left set 3", right set 2.75". $25-35. Note slight difference in size of bodies.

Pheasants with tails down. 2.75". $75-85.

Golden pheasants. 2.75". $125-150.

Striding roosters. 4". $125-150. No hens have
been found to date.

Striding rooster hors d'oeuvres holder.
4.75". $70-80.

Left set, California quail. 2.5". $65-
75. Right set, Bob White quail. 2.75".
$45-55.

Pigs. 4". $90-100.

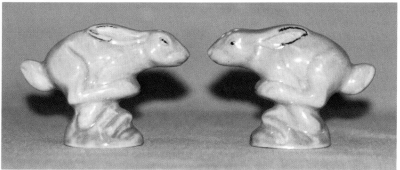

Rabbits. 2". $90-100.

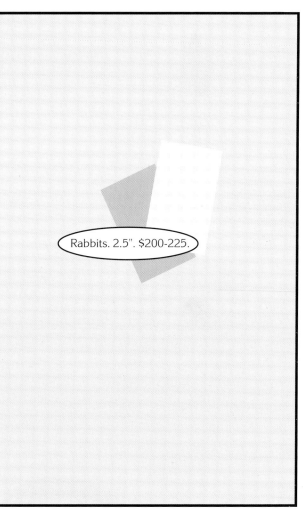

Rabbits. 2.5". $200-225.

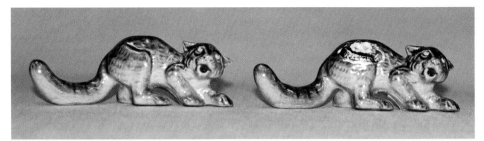

Pumas. 1.5". $450-500.

Raccoons. 2". $150-175.

Roadrunners. 2.5". $150-175.

Miniature turkeys. 1.5". $150-175.

Turkeys. 3". $55-65.

Skunks. 1.75". $50-60.

Skunks. 2.5". $45-55.

Skunks. 3". $45-55.

Swans. 2.25". $50-60.

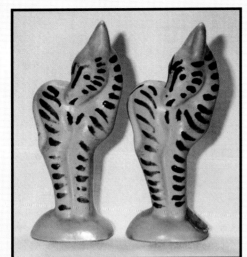

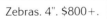
Zebras. 4". $800+.

Prairie roses. .5". $40-50.

Prairie roses with gold trim. .5". Rare,
museum piece. Not priced.

Cactus. Left set, Pincushion.
1". $45-55. Right set 1.25".
$65-75.

Cactus. Outside set, Devil's
Finger. 2.5". $100-125. Middle
set 1.75". $75-85.

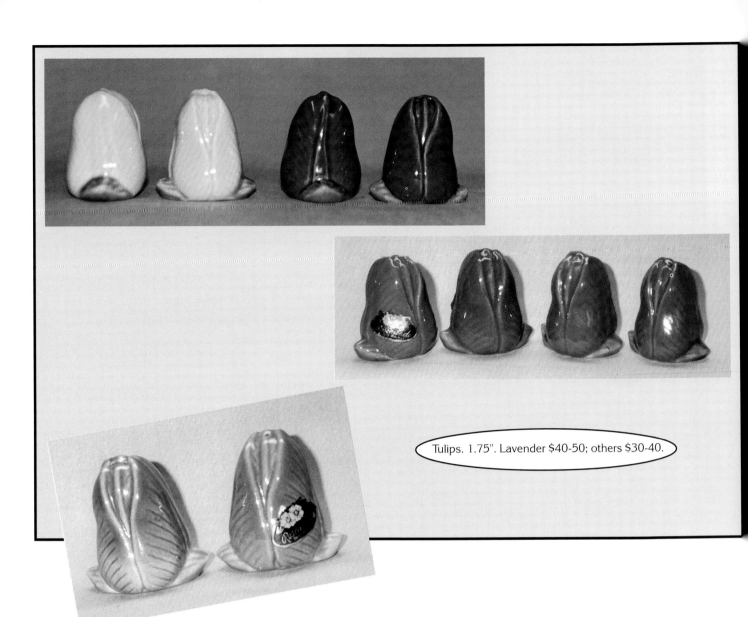

Tulips. 1.75". Lavender $40-50; others $30-40.

Tulips shown with spoon rest.

Paul Bunyan and Babe. 2.25". $100-125.

Indian heads. 2.5". $400+.

Fort Lincoln. 2". $600+. This set has a look-out tower on top. The Fort Abercrombie set, which we were unable to photograph, does not have a tower.

Log cabins. 1.25". $600+.

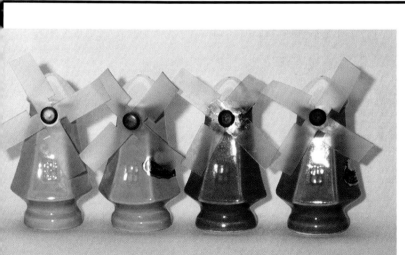

Windmills. 3". $100-125.

69

Sailboats. 3.25". $275-300.

Sailboats with silver trim for 25th anniversary. 3.25". $300+.

Sailboats with gold trim for 50th anniversary. 3.25". $300+.

Sailboats with incised letters "City of Lakes" and raised letters "Minneapolis, Minn". 3.25". $300+.

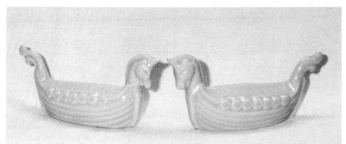

Viking ships. 1.75". $300-325.

Boxing gloves. 2.25". $350+.

Boxing gloves. 2.25". Decorated
by a school child. Not priced.

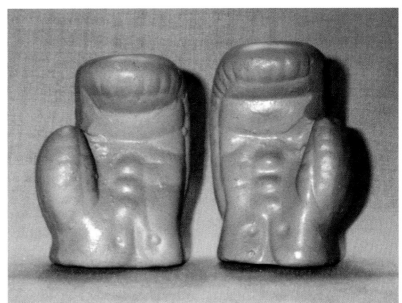

International Peace Garden monument. 1.75".
$275-300.

Geographical Center of North America
monument, Rugby, North Dakota. 4.25".
$350+.

"Indian 'God of Peace' St. Paul, Minn." in raised
letters. 4". $450+.

"Indian 'God of Peace' Saint Paul, Minnesota" in raised letters. 6.75". $450+.

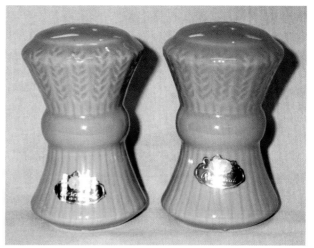

Shocks of wheat. 3.75". $125-150.

Balls on pedestals. 3". $35-45.

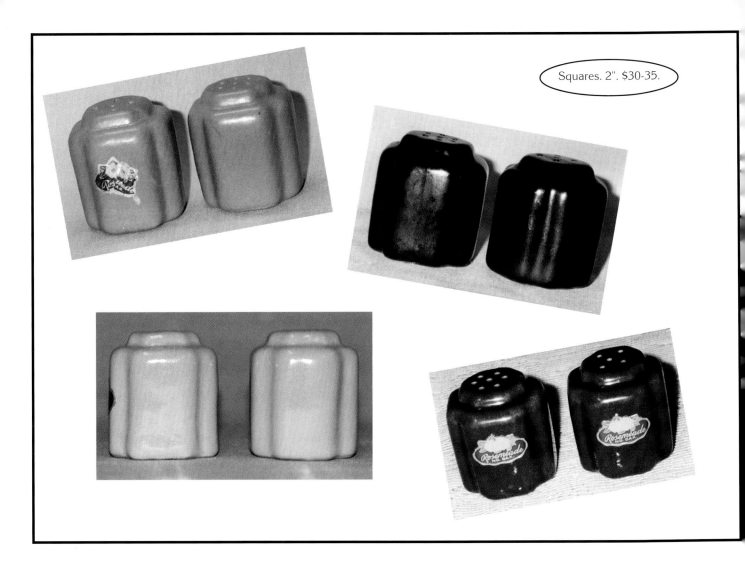

Swirl. Large set 7". $75-100. Single with one hole probably used on a bar to put salt in beer. 4". Not priced.

Hourglass shape. 4.5". One pair and three singles. $35-45 pr.

Bulb shape. 5". $75-85.

Range type. 5". $45-55.

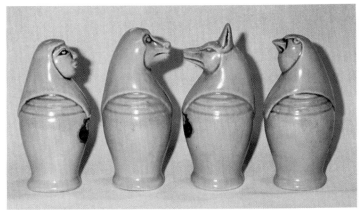

Canopic jars. 3.25". $600+.
Front and side views.

Canopic jars. 3.25". $600+.

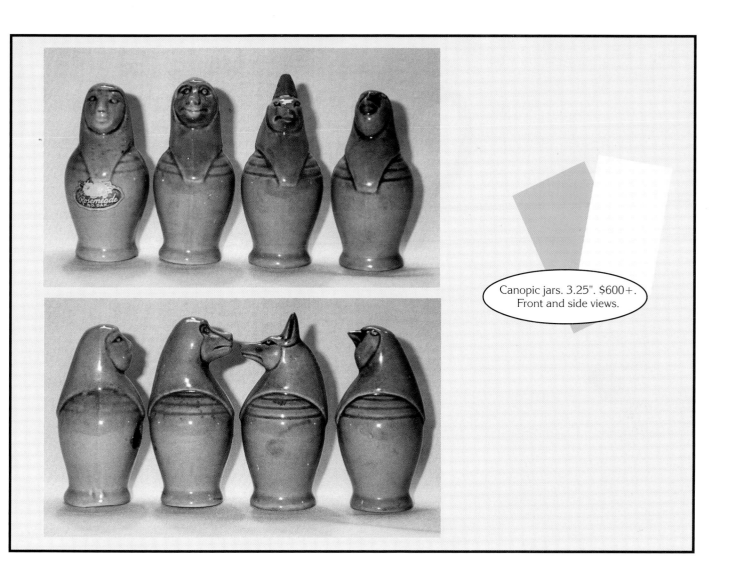

Canopic jars. 3.25". $600+.
Front and side views.

Canopic jars. 3.25". $600+.

Cucumbers. 1.75". $25-30.

Cucumber singles. 1.75". Left, white clay; right, North Dakota clay. Shows difference in clay. Not priced.

Cucumber singles. 1.75". White clay. $30-35 if pr.

Brussels sprouts. 1.75". Corn. 2.25". $25-30 each. Note: Corn also found with separate corn ashtray not issued with the set.

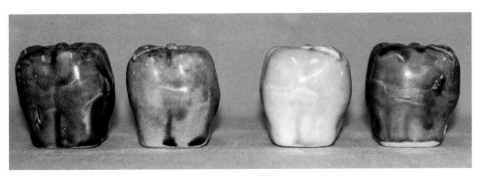

Peppers. 1.75". Left set, North Dakota clay. $25-30. Right singles: one white clay, one North Dakota clay. Not priced.

Potatoes. 2". $200-225.

Potatoes. 2". Shown with spoon rest.

Potatoes. Left set 1.5". $175-200. Right set 1". $400+.

Potatoes incised "Compliments of L. E. Tibert Co." 2". $225-250.

Potatoes with raised letters "N. Dak. State Seed Dep't." 2". $225-250.

Anthropomorphic bowling pins, incised "King Pin Foods." 4.5". $500+.

Corn with raised letters "Trojan." 5". $250-275.

Black Angus shown on ashtray has also been made as salt and pepper shakers. 2". $500+ pr. of shakers.

Chef shown on ashtray has also been made as salt and pepper shakers. 3.5". $500+ pr. of shakers.

Messer

Joe and Eunice Messer designed and produced their pottery line in Bowman, North Dakota from the early 1950s to 1956. Among the numerous types of items made were salt and pepper shakers. These included farm animals, wildlife, national landmarks, and advertising.

Prairie dogs. 2.25". $225-250.

Rabbits. 1". $275-300. Stamped "Cpyrt 1953."

Rabbits. 1". $275-300. Incised "(c) 1953."

Rabbit single. 1".
$275-300 if pr.

Seals. 2". $300-325.

Hereford bull and cow. 3". $475-500.

Black Angus calves. 1". $300-325.

Holstein and Hereford calves. 1". $300-325.

Ghosts. 3". $475-500.

Devils Tower. 2.25". $300-325. Made for 50th anniversary of opening the monument.

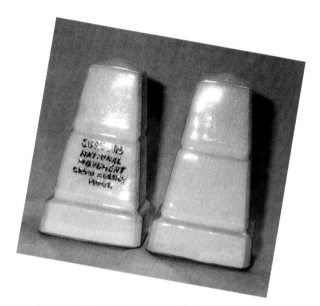

Custers National Monument. 3". $400-425.

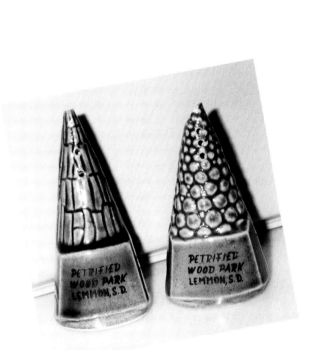

Petrified Wood Park. 3.5". $350-375.

Oil wells. $350-375.

Kildeer Equity grain elevators. 3.25".
$125-150.

Farmers Equity Union grain
elevators. 3.25". $100-125.

L.V. Duncanson grain elevators.
3.25". $125-150.

Frontier gas pumps. 3.25". $250-275.

Farmers Union gas
pumps. 3.5". $200-225.

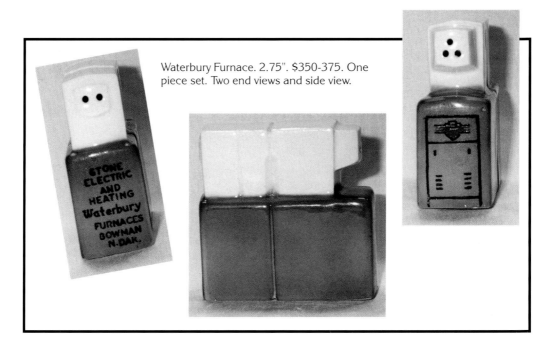

Waterbury Furnace. 2.75". $350-375. One
piece set. Two end views and side view.

Checkerboard Cafe chefs. 4.25". $350-375.

Little Heart Ceramics

In the late 1950s, after Messer ceased production, Joe Messer sold several molds to L & H Mfg Co. of Mandan, North Dakota. Commercially available and company designed molds were also used. Methods of identification included a small heart label, free hand or ink stamp, and raised lettering. Production ceased in 1968. Sets shown here are from Messer molds.

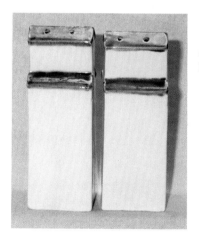

Grain elevators. 3.25".
Heart label. $75-85.

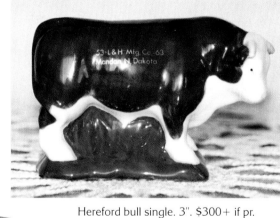

Hereford bull single. 3". $300+ if pr.

Oil wells. 3.75". $90-100.

Dickota

Named for Dickinson, North Dakota, this pottery company operated in the 1930s. The various marks used all contain the Dickota name.

Cableware design. 1.75". $35-45.

North Dakota School of Mines (UND)

In the early 1900s, the Ceramic Department was established under the direction of Margaret Cable. Various artware has been produced through the years by both instructors and students. Pieces were marked with a stamp showing the University name until 1963. Since then, only a student's signature appears.

Owls. 2.5". $65-75.

Tulips. 1.75". $55-65.

California Potteries

Sascha Brastoff

From 1947 to 1963, Sascha Brastoff headed a ceramics business in Los Angeles. Using new and unusual materials, a flamboyant style of decoration, and substantial gold trim, he produced unique designs. While all pieces made were signed, only those with a full name were personally crafted by Brastoff; the others were usually produced under his supervision. Although his salt and peppers are beautiful, we have seen few figural ones to date.

Horses. 3.5". $75-85.

Winter lodge. 4". $40-50.

Eskimos. 4". $45-55.

Huskies. 4". $45-55.

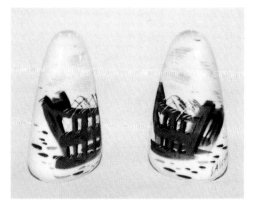

Dog sleds. 4". $40-50.

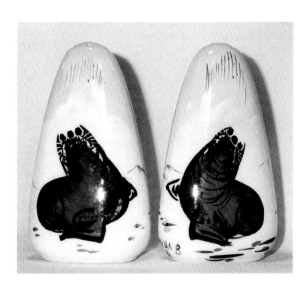

Walrus. 4". $45-55.

Mountain and iceberg. 4". $40-50.

Unconfirmed Brastoff fish on tails. 4.5". $45-55.

Matthew Adams

Matthew Adams was a protégé of Sascha Brastoff. In the 1950s, Brastoff was asked to design an "Alaska" ceramic line; Adams painted this line. After leaving Brastoff's company, Adams was given approval to continue producing "Alaska" items. The location of his studio is unknown, although it may have been in Alaska. His pieces are signed Matthew or Matt Adams. The shakers located to date are not figural.

Seals. 3.75". $55-65.

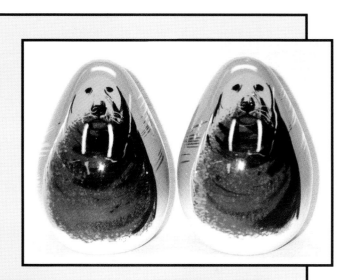

Walrus. 3.75". $55-65.

Iceberg single. 3.75". $50-60 if pr.

Polar bears. 3.75". $55-65.

Moose single. 3.75". $55-65 if pr.

Polar bears. 5.25". $65-75.

Kodiak bears. 5.25". $65-75.

90

Eskimos. 3.75". $55-65.

Igloo. 3.75". $50-60.

Two igloos. 3.75". $50-60.

Three igloos. 5.25". $60-70.

Lane and Co.

Lane and Co. operated in Southern California in the 1950s and 1960s and are best known for TV lamps/planters. This salt and pepper set is the only one known to date produced by this company.

Indians. 3.75". $250+. Shows mark on bottom.

Jean Manley

Jean Manley was a California ceramist in the 1940s best known for her doll-like figurines.

Reba Rookwood

These sets are stamped "Reba Rookwood Pottery, Pasadena, Calif." or "Reba Rookwood Pottery." We were unable to find any further information on this company.

People. 4.25". $85-95.

Pig couple. 3.75". $25-35.

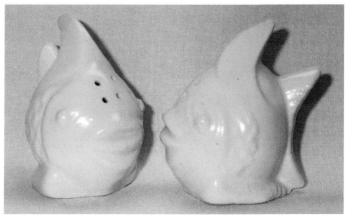

Fish. 3". $10-20.

Poinsettia Studios

This company was located in California, probably in the 1950s. Numerous attempts to obtain information from various California agencies and libraries, as well as other reference sources, have met with no success.

Original box for the Little Miss Muffet set.

Aladdin and his lamp. 3.25". $80-90.

King Midas and pot of gold.
3.25". $80-90.

Hare and tortoise. 3.5". $80-90.

Little Miss Muffet. 2.5". $65-75.

Little Red Hen and loaf of bread. 3.5". $80-90.

Little Red Riding Hood. 3.5". $80-90.

Old Mother Hubbard. 3.5". $65-75.

Mary Had a Little Lamb. 3.5". $65-75.

Old Woman in the Shoe. 3.5". $65-75.

Peter, Peter Pumpkin Eater and his wife. 3.5". $70-80.

Wee Willie Winkle. 3.5". $70-80.

Flower the Skunk. 3.5". $80-90.

Circus wagon and horse. 2.75". $70-80.

Rabbit in the hat. 4.5". $70-80.

Birds on tree stumps. 3.25. $30-40.

Anthropomorphic trains (Little Engine that Could). 2". $80-90.
Both eyes open, both eyes closed, one eye open and one closed.

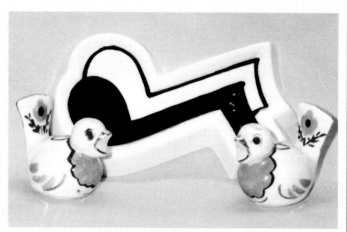

Birds with their note
tray. 2". $50-60.

Cats on pillows. 3.75". $35-45.

Cats on rug. 2.75". $40-50. Shown on their rug and with three different rugs.

Chicken and polka dot/solid color egg. 2". $30-40.

Chicken and gold/solid color egg shown with a tray. 2". $40-50. Not sure if this tray was issued with these sets.

Chicken and polka dot/solid color egg. 2". $30-40.

Chicken and egg shown in egg cups.

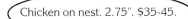

Chicken on nest. 2.75". $35-45.

Crows on or beside their two corn trays. 3.25". $40-50.

Ducks on oval tray with cattails. 2.75". $45-55.

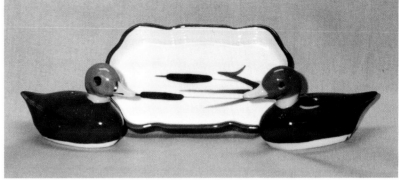

Ducks on oblong tray with cattails. 2.5". $45-55.

Pelicans with two and three holes shown without their tray. 2.5". $30-40.

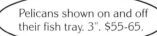
Pelicans shown on and off their fish tray. 3". $55-65.

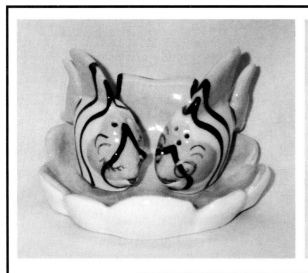

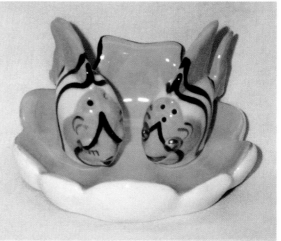

Fish on their shell trays. 2.25". $50-60.

Strutting pigeons. 2.25". $40-50.

Strutting pigeons beside a tray. 2.25". $45-55.

Donkeys. 2.5". $50-60.

Elephants. 1.5". $50-60.

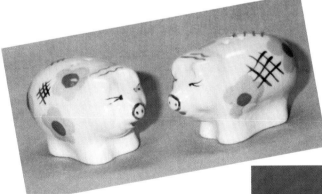

Pigs in their fence tray. 2". $55-65.

Pigs without their fence tray. 1.5". $30-40.

Pigs outside their fence tray. 2". $55-65.

Children in and outside their peanut tray. 2.75". $90-100.

Cowboy and cowgirl with their wagon wheel tray. 3.75". $55-65.

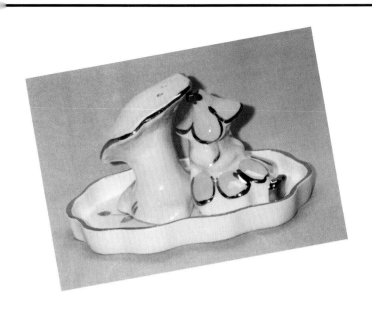

Elves and mushrooms in their trays. 2.5". $60-70.

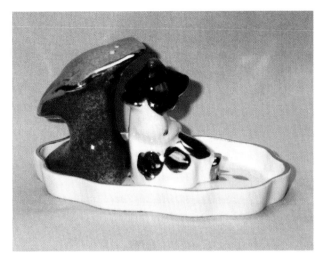

Santa and Mrs. Claus. 3.5". $90-100.

Snow people and snowman single. 2.75". $60-70 pr.

Flowers in basket. 2.25". $35-45.

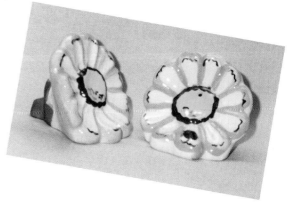

Daisies with lady bug. 2.25". $25-35.

Coffee pot and tea kettle shown with their heart shaped tray. 2.5". $30-40.

Coffee pot and tea kettle shown with an oblong tray. 2.5". $25-35.

Coffee pot on trivet. 3.5".
$25-35. Front and back views.

Coffee pot on trivet. 3.5". $25-35.

Coffee pot on trivet. 3.5".
$25-35. Front and back views.

Coffee pots shown on and off their shelf tray. 2.75". $25-35.

Stacked lamp. 4". $25-35.

Lamps shown on and off their shelf tray. 3.5". $25-35.

Cookbooks shown with their bowl tray. 2.5". $35-45.

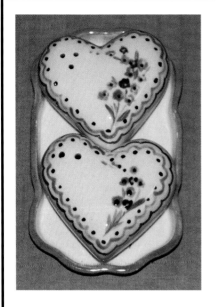

Hearts shown on and off their tray. 1.25". $35-45.

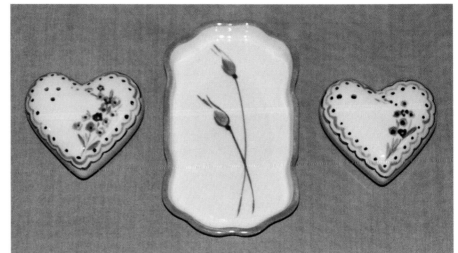

Iron and stove shown with a tray. 2.5". $30-40.

Coffee grinder and cracker barrel. 2.25". $30-40.

Pots with corn on top, probably singles. 1.75". $25-35 if pr.

Butter churn and milk pail shown with their tray. 2.75". $35-45.

Outhouse single. 2.5" $30-40 if pr. Front and back views.

High button shoes. 2.5". $35-45.

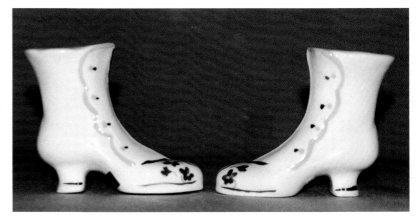

Silo and barn. 3". $30-40.

Floral design. 4.5". $25-35.

Barnware

These sets were made by Vera LaFountain Dunn of Hollywood, California in the mid-1940s.

"Hansel and Gretel." 5". $35-40.

Label "Hansel & Gretel, California Original."

"Hilda and Pepicheck." 5.75". $35-40.

Kay Finch

Kay Finch and her husband Braden started Kay Finch Ceramics in Santa Ana, California in 1938. This company became one of the leading figural potteries in the world. Although she designed a variety of items, it appears animals, especially dogs, were her favorite. Her work is distinctive, combining animated form and hand painted linear detail, often with applied flowers and ceramic curls. The studio closed in 1963 after Braden's death.

"Puss" and "Pup." 6". $450+.

Horse heads. 5". $275-300.

Owls. 3.75". $175-200.

Squares with flowers. 1.75". $100-125.

Penguins. 3.25". $275-300.

Turkeys. 3.5". $175-200.

Sorcha Boru

California ceramist Claire Stewart used the name Sorcha Boru professionally. She had a ceramic studio from 1932 until 1955. Her colorful, slip decorated products include many salt and peppers, most of which are hand incised "S B", "S B C", or "S B S" with a copyright insignia.

Bears. 2.5". $20-30.

Bears. 2.5". $30-40. Unglazed with aqua glaze trim.

Bears. 2.5". $20-30.

Bear single. 2.5". $25-35 if pr.

Turkeys. 2.25". $25-35.

Birds, yellow pair and three singles. 2.25". $20-30 pr.

Pekingese dogs. 2". $30-40.

Cats. 2.75". $40-50.

Hen and rooster. 4". $35-45.

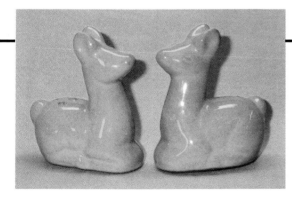

Deer. 2.5". $35-45.

Elephants with Shriner hats. 2.75". $50-60.

Hippo single. 1.75". $40-50 if pr.

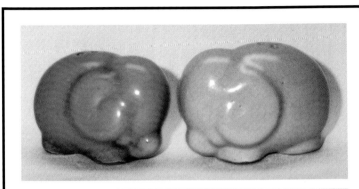

Elephants. 1.5". $35-45 pr. Two singles and two pairs.

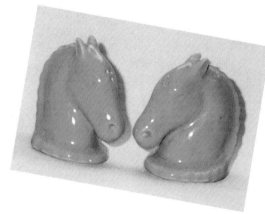

Horse heads. 2.5". $35-45.

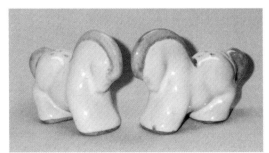
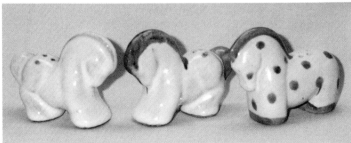

Horses. 1.75". $35-45.

Horses. 3.5". $50-60.

Koalas. 3.25". $50-60.

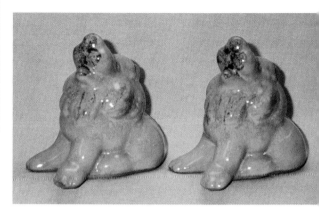

Lions. 3". $50-60.

Mice. 2.5". $20-30.

Owls. 2.5". $25-35.

Pigs. 2.25". $20-30.

Rabbits. 3.25". $25-35 pr. Three pairs
and gray with mauve trim singles.

Seahorses. 4.25". $50-60.

Lambs. 2.5". $25-35.

Squirrels. 2.75". $25-35.

Flower girls. 3.25". $50-60.

Flower girls. 4". $55-65.

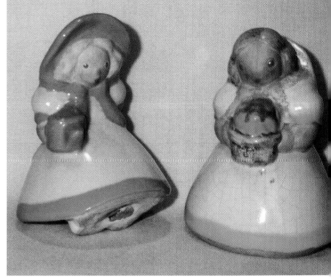

Mary, Mary Quite Contrary. 3.5". $85-95 pr. Two pairs, one single with flowers.

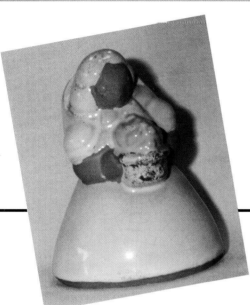

Angel single. 5.25".
$65-75 if pr.

Mary, Mary sugar
shaker. $35-45.

124

Cook and maid. 6". $75-85.

"Topsy" single.
5.5". $85-95 if pr.

Boy with girl at water fountain. 5.25". $65-75.

Girl at water fountain single. 3".
$65-75 if pr.

Boy and two girls with different trim. 5.25". $65-75.
Same boy goes with either girl to form proper set.

Gardening children. 4". $65-75. Two pairs and single boy.

Little Boy Blue and Little Bo Peep. 3.5". $85-95. One set with Bo Peep in curls, one set without curls.

Kissing kids shown apart and together. 3.75". $55-65.

Kissing kids. 3.75". $55-65.

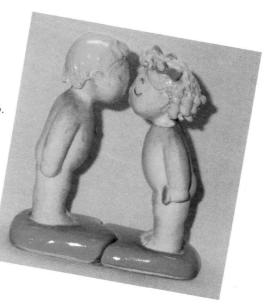

"Little Eva" single. 5.5". $65-75 if pr.

Mexican couple. 2.75". $50-60.

Dutch boy with girl. 5". $65-75.

Boating couples. Left set 3.5", right set 3.75". $85-95.

Fox huntsmen. 5.25". $85-95.

Skiers. 4.25". Ice skaters. 4.75". $85-95 each.

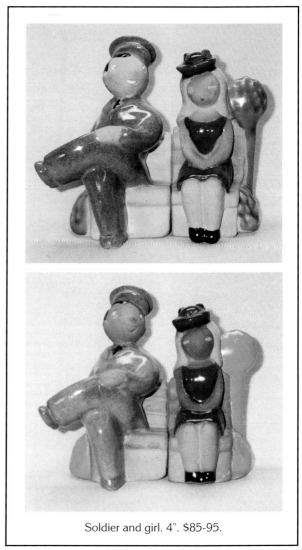

Soldier and girl. 4". $85-95.

Sailor and girl. 5.5". $85-95.

Sailor and lady of the night, plus single sailor. 3.5". $85-95 pr.

King and Queen. 5". $85-95.

Clowns. 4.5". $90-100.

"Timothy" and "Effie Mae" incised. 2.5". $70-80.

Hawaiian couple. 4.5". $85-95.

Cowboys. 4". $85-95.

132

Bride and groom. 4.5". $85-95.

Bride and groom. 4.25". $75-85.

Brayton Laguna

Founded by Durlin Brayton in 1927 at his Laguna Beach, California home, the Brayton Laguna Pottery became one of the foremost Southern California pottery companies. It was the first pottery licensed by Walt Disney Studios to produce ceramic portrayals of Disney animated characters. Various factors led to the pottery's closing in 1968. Today the former facilities serve as the Laguna Art Center.

Both Pages
Chef and cook. 5.5". $75-85.
Note variations in color of spoons and trims.

Alice in Wonderland and the Walrus. 4.25". $225-250.

Humpty Dumpty. 3.5". $100-125.

King and Queen of Hearts. 4". $150-175.

Butler and maid. 5.25". $200-225.

Lady single. 7.25".
$150-175 if pr.

Provincial peasant couple. 5.5". $40-50.
Front and back views.

137

Provincial peasant couple. 5.5".
$40-50. Front and back views.

Provincial peasant couple. 5.5".
$40-50. Note different trims.

Tweedle Dee and Tweedle Dum. 3.75".
$150-175.

People. 4.75". $40-50.

139

Couple. 5". $65-75.

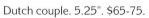

Dutch couple. 5.25". $65-75.

Couple. 4.5". $65-75.

Couple. 5.5". $50-60.

Clown and dog. 6.75". $80-90.

Gingham dog and calico cat. 4.25". $40-50.

Rooster and hen. 5". $50-60.

Lions. 2.25". $40-50.
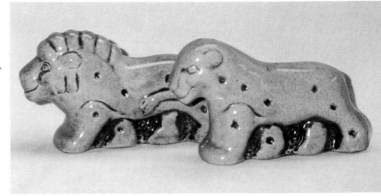

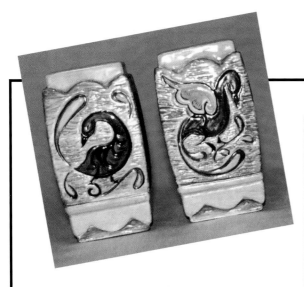

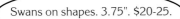
Swans on shapes. 3.75". $20-25.

Maridan

No information has been located on this company. The only marking is a black label with gold script letters, found on some of these sets. As no country of origin is indicated, we believe this to be an American company, probably located in California, operating as many others did in the 1940s-1950s. Some sets probably mix and match.

Mary and her lamb. 3.75". $40-50.

The Big Bad Wolf and one Pig in straw house. 4". $75-85.

The Fox and the Grapes. 3.5". $30-40.

Jack in the box. 6". $35-45.

Angels. 4.5". $35-45.

Children. 3.25". $40-50.

Choir children. 3.5". $35-45.

Courting couple. 3.5". $35-45.

Cowboy on horse. 4". $35-45.

Panda with tree trunk. 3.5". $30-40.

Hen with chicks on hen house. 4". $30-40.

Panda with tree trunk. 3.5". $30-40.

Elephants. 4". $30-40.

Kangaroo and baby in pouch. 4".
$35-45.

Squirrels. 2.75". $35-45.

Koala with tree trunk. 3.5". $30-40.

Lion on circus stand. 4.25".
$35-45

Lion and lamb. 2.75". $35-45.

Rhumba dancer rabbits. 4.25". $35-45.

Rabbit couple with carrot. 4.5". $35-45.

Rabbit couple. 4.5". $35-45.

Rabbit with various signs. 3.5". $30-40.

Squirrels in trees. 4.25". $35-45.

Snails. 2". $35-45.

Gifts. 2.25". $20-30.

Trash can and basket.
3.5". $20-30.

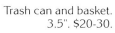

Ceramic Arts Studio

Ceramic Arts Studio (CAS) operated in Madison, Wisconsin from 1941 to 1955, with Betty Harrington as the leading designer. For further information, please reference the CAS books listed in the Bibliography. We are primarily including salt and pepper sets not pictured in these references.

Among the CAS products are unmarked fish made as both figurines and shakers. These were called swish and swirl, or twist-tail and straight-tail. Examples were included in a display at the first CAS convention, held in 1996. Several sets were shown to Betty Harrington and her daughter by Sylvia at this time and Betty verified these as being CAS. She stated that all pieces were made with three holes and that two of a kind were the proper pair. She explained further that these could be identified by the sheen on the bottom, caused by placing each piece on a thin layer of oil when removed from the kiln. This process resulted in a lack of glaze at the very bottom edge.

Purple cow lap sitter. 5". $350+. Rare.

Black bear lap sitter. 4.5". $400+. Rare.

"Waldo and Sassy." 1.25". $225-250.

"Peek and Boo." 4". $250-275.

Kitten and pitcher. 2.5". $125-150.
Note different color pitchers.

Brown and white spaniels.
2.5". $175-200.

Stylized doe and fawn. 4". $90-100.

All white Santa Claus and tree. 2". $200-225.

Wee Indians. 3.25". $65-75.
Note gray body color.

"Wing-Sang" and "Lu-Tang."
6.25". $350+.

Sultan and kneeling harem girl. 5". $300+.

Fish head up and fish
head down. 3.5". $65-75.

Bottom of twist-tail fish.

Straight-tail and twist-tail singles. Not priced.

Both Pages
Swish or Twist-tail Fish. 2".
$25-35. Add $10 for gold trim.

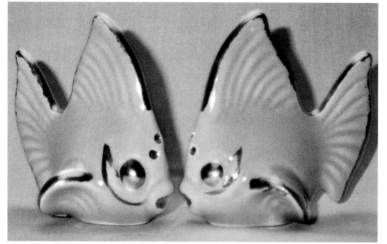

Both Pages
Swirl or Straight-tail Fish. 3.25".
$30-40. Add $10 for gold trim.

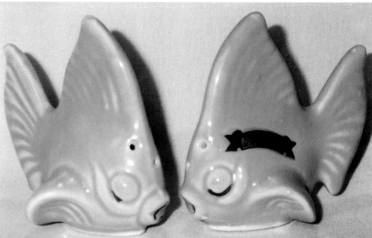

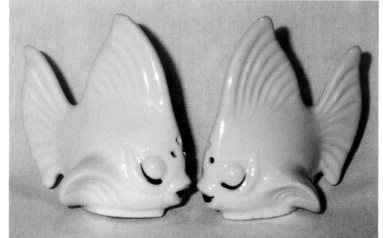

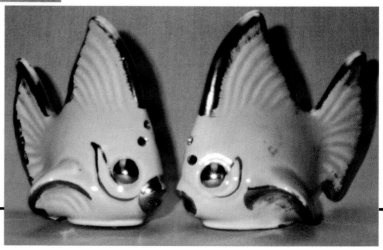

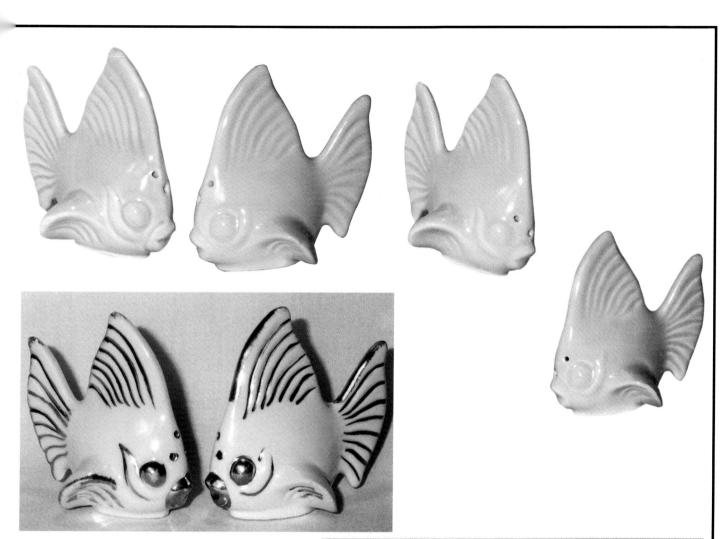

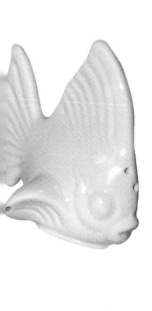

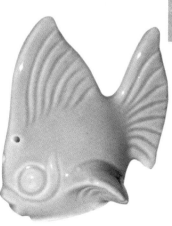

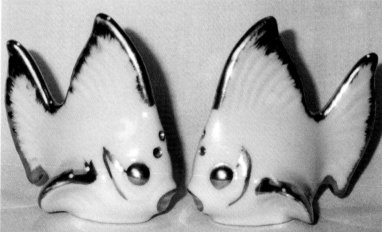

Bibliography

Bakken, Bill. *Rosemeade Price Guide, Fourth Edition.* September 1999.

Chipman, Jack. *Collector's Encyclopedia of California Pottery, Second Edition.* Paducah, KY: Collector Books, 1999.

Conti, Steve, Bethany, A. DeWane, and Seay, Bill. *Collector's Encyclopedia of Sascha Brastoff.* Paducah, KY: Collector Books, 1995.

Dommel, Darlene Hurst. *Collector's Encyclopedia of the Dakota Potteries.* Paducah, KY: Collector Books, 1996.

Frick, Devin, Frick, Jean, and Martinez, Richard. *Collectible Kay Finch.* Paducah, KY: Collector Books, 1997.

Harms, Irene J. and Sampson, Shirley B. *Beautiful Rosemeade.* Garretson, SD: Sanders Printing Co., 1986.

Huxford, Sharon and Bob. *Schroeder's Antiques Price Guide, Seventeenth and Eighteenth Editions.* Paducah, KY: Collector Books, 1999 and 2000.

Laumbach, Sabra Olson. *Harrington Figurines.* Hillsdale, MI: Ferguson Communications, 1985.

Schneider, Mike. *California Potteries.* Atglen, PA: Schiffer Publishing Ltd., 1995.

Schneider, Mike. *Ceramic Arts Studio.* Atglen, PA: Schiffer Publishing Ltd., 1994.

Wiege, Jim, Spencer, Audrey and Darrell. *Little Heart Ceramics.* 1999.